HITTING THE BOOKS
Skills for Reading, Writing, and Research

Studying and Test Taking

Nina Simone Mosley

Rourke
Educational Media

rourkeeducationalmedia.com

Scan for Related Titles and Teacher Resources

Before Reading:

Building Academic Vocabulary and Background Knowledge

Before reading a book, it is important to tap into what your child or students already know about the topic. This will help them develop their vocabulary, increase their reading comprehension, and make connections across the curriculum.

1. *Look at the cover of the book. What will this book be about?*
2. *What do you already know about the topic?*
3. *Let's study the Table of Contents. What will you learn about in the book's chapters?*
4. *What would you like to learn about this topic? Do you think you might learn about it from this book? Why or why not?*
5. *Use a reading journal to write about your knowledge of this topic. Record what you already know about the topic and what you hope to learn about the topic.*
6. *Read the book.*
7. *In your reading journal, record what you learned about the topic and your response to the book.*
8. *After reading the book complete the activities below.*

Content Area Vocabulary
Read the list. What do these words mean?

anxious
clarify
concentrate
distractions
effective
extracurricular
focus
nutritious
relaxed
self-esteem
strategies
stress

After Reading:

Comprehension and Extension Activity

After reading the book, work on the following questions with your child or students in order to check their level of reading comprehension and content mastery.

1. *What are some things you can do to make test taking less stressful? (Asking Questions)*
2. *If you waited until the last minute to prepare for a test, do you think you would do as well as if you prepared? (Infer)*
3. *How might you feel before taking a big test? (Text to self connection)*
4. *Give some examples of what a good study environment would be like. (Summarize)*
5. *When you walk into class to take a test, what are the first things you should do? (Visualize)*

Extension Activity

You have a big math test next week. You are really nervous and not sure where to start preparing. Make a list of all the helpful hints in the book and follow them. If you are unsure of some of the material, ask the teacher if he/she may have a study guide you can use. Now, concentrate and find a quiet place to study. When you ace the test, share your grade with your classmates and maybe you can help someone who didn't do as well with the strategy you used.

Table of Contents

Great Habits That Last a Lifetime

Have you noticed your school to-do list getting longer? With each grade, homework assignments get tougher, workloads get bigger, and tests get harder.

If you feel overwhelmed, you're not alone. But knowing proper study tips and test taking **strategies** can make schoolwork feel manageable. With the right skills, you will be able to approach every challenge with a positive attitude.

Students who don't know how to study have a difficult time succeeding in school.

Smarter Studying

Improving your study skills will make it easier to learn and do well in class. The right way to study may be different for each student. Some students find it easiest to study right after school. Others prefer to study in the same quiet place every day. You just have to figure out what works for you.

Study Tip

Good studying starts in class. When you pay attention in class, you are starting the process of learning and studying. Find a good seat that is far away from any **distractions** and gives you a good view of the board.

Taking good notes in school means easier studying at home. Write down important things that your teacher talks about in class. Use good handwriting so you can read your notes later.

At home, make sure that you give yourself enough time to study and do your homework. If you wait too long to start your work, you will have a long night ahead of you. Your work will also be sloppy. Make sure you do your best by planning ahead.

Keep a calendar by your study area and write down your tests and assignment due dates. Use the calendar to track your **extracurricular** activities too. This way, you will know when you are free to study.

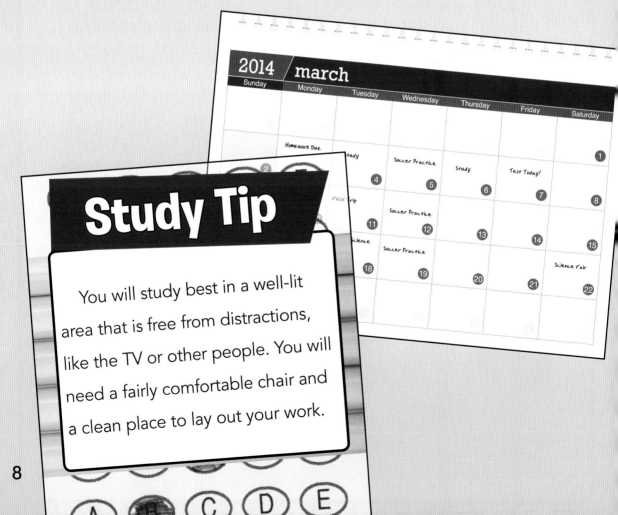

Study Tip

You will study best in a well-lit area that is free from distractions, like the TV or other people. You will need a fairly comfortable chair and a clean place to lay out your work.

If you have a lot to do, it can help to break your work into smaller chunks. **Focus** on one subject at a time. Don't worry if you can't remember something on the first try. The more time you spend reviewing something, the more likely you are to remember it.

Study Tip

Short breaks help you **concentrate**. When you work on something for a long time, you may start thinking about other things. Get up and do something else. Then come back to your studying. You should be ready to focus again.

Test Preparation

It may seem like no matter what grade or school you are in, you are always taking tests. And if taking tests causes you a lot of icky feelings, you are not alone. Even students who do great in school can have trouble when it comes to testing.

By preparing for a test, you can go into an exam with confidence. Test-taking can be a lot easier if you pick up some useful habits and test preparation skills.

Before a test you may feel:

- Trouble concentrating
- Low **self-esteem**
- **Anxious** or nervous
- Stomach problems
- Trouble sleeping
- Sweaty or cold hands

Start early. Start studying several days before the test. This will give you more time to learn and remember the information you need to know. Cramming the night before will increase your **stress**. Spend more time studying the most important information.

If you don't know what is most important, ask your teacher. He or she may even have a study guide for you to use!

Make study sheets by summarizing the main ideas in a few points. Make a single page of notes and review them several times.

For math tests, redo any homework problems you missed. Make certain that you understand where you went wrong the first time.

Preparing for a big test doesn't end with studying. Be sure to get a good night's sleep and eat a **nutritious** breakfast before heading to school. When you take care of your body by eating right and getting enough sleep, you will be able to do your best.

Don't stay up all night studying the night before a test. Students who get a good night's sleep before a test do better than people who pull all-nighters.

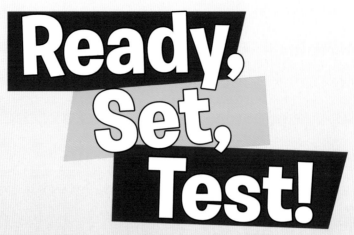

Ready, Set, Test!

Get the test off to the best possible start by getting there on time. Arriving late will make you feel rushed and nervous. Try to arrive at least five minutes before the test so you can go into the test **relaxed**.

TEST TIME

Take a deep breath. Do your best to stay relaxed and calm. No matter what grade you get, when you have studied hard you know that you will have done your best.

Bring any materials that you need for the test, such as pencils, pens, a calculator, erasers, and paper. It's a good idea to bring at least 2 pencils or pens.

When you get the test, read the instructions carefully. If you skip the instructions, you could miss important information. Read each question so that you understand what it's asking. If you don't understand a question, ask your teacher to **clarify** what it's asking.

It's important not to get distracted and take your mind off the test.

Keep focused on your own work. If you spend time worrying about what everyone else is doing, you are not paying enough attention to your own work. Remember that you have prepared for the test and are ready to do your best.

Answer each question carefully and make sure not to rush. If you move through the test too quickly, you are likely to make a careless mistake.

You also don't want to waste time thinking too much about one question. If you come to a question you don't know the answer to, skip over it. Circle the question so you know to come back to it later. You may even come up with the answer to the hard question while you are answering an easier one.

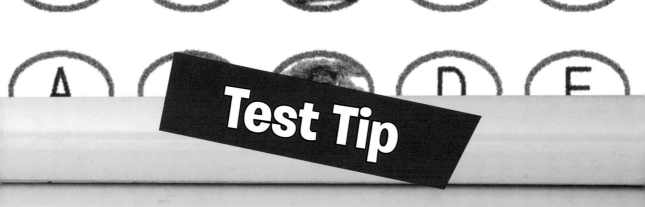

If you finish the test before time is up, go back over the questions, especially the ones that seemed hard. Check your work. Fixing mistakes can help boost your grade.

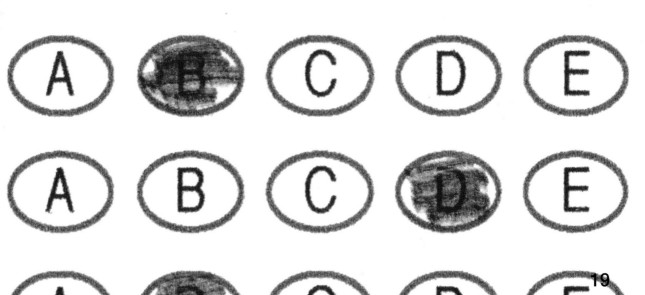

Once the test is over, try not to think about it for a while. Instead of worrying about what grade you will get, reward yourself for making it through the test. Enjoy the fact that you are finished!

Effective study strategies and test preparation will help you on your path toward school success. When you know how to study and prepare for a test, you can go into each class ready to show off what you've learned.

Glossary

anxious (ANGK-shuhs): worried

clarify (KLAR-uh-fye): to explain something more clearly

concentrate (KAHN-suhn-trate): to give all of your thought and attention to something

distractions (di-STRAKT-shuhns): something that makes it hard to pay attention

effective (i-FEK-tiv): something that works well and gets the job done

extracurricular (EK-struh-kuh-RIK-yuh-luhr): extra activities (such as sports) outside of regular school

focus (FOH-kuhs): concentrating on the task at hand

nutritious (noo-TRISH-uhs): containing substances that help you stay healthy and strong

relaxed (ri-LAKST): to become less tense, anxious, or strained

self-esteem (self-i-STEEM): a feeling of personal pride and of respect for yourself

strategies (STRAT-i-jees): smart plans to meet a goal or solve a problem

stress (stres): mental or emotional strain or pressure

Index

Websites to Visit

www.kidshealth.org/kid/feeling/school/studying.html#

www.testtakingtips.com/study

www.studygs.net/tsttak1.htm

About the Author

Nina Simone Mosley lives in Atlanta, Georgia. As a teacher, she always provided her kids with the necessary tools to be successful in school. She encourages kids to study hard and effectively prepare for their academic success!

Meet The Author!
www.meetREMauthors.com

www.rourkeeducationalmedia.com

PHOTO CREDITS: Cover © Aldo Mirillo; title page, 21 © Lisa F. Young; page 3, 15 © 89studio, turtix; page 5 ©Kamira; page 6 © Solphoto; page 7, 8, 9, 15, 19 © R. MACKAY PHOTOGRAPHY, LLC, www.delightimages.com; page 9 © visualhunter, page 10 © Rodolfo Arguedas; page 11 © clerkenwell; page 12 © Elena Elisseeva; page 13 © FPWing; page 14 © zaptik; page 16 © monkeybusinessimages; page 17 © GlobalStock; page 18 © Syda Productions; page 20 © wond yu liang

Edited by: Jill Sherman

Cover Design by: Jen Thomas

Interior Design by: Rhea Magaro

Library of Congress PCN Data

Studying and Test Taking /Nina Simone Mosley
(Hitting the Books: Skills for Reading, Writing, and Research)
ISBN (hard cover) (alk. paper) 978-1-62717-688-0
ISBN (soft cover) 978-1-62717-810-5
ISBN (e-Book) 978-1-62717-925-6
Library of Congress Control Number: 2014935482

Rourke Educational Media
Printed in the United States of America,
North Mankato, Minnesota

Also Available as:

ROURKE'S
e-Books